Katharina Deserno

Mein erstes Konzert

My First Concert

25 leichte Vortragsstücke aus 5 Jahrhunderten
25 Easy Concert Pieces from 5 Centuries

für Violoncello und Klavier
for Violoncello and Piano

ED 22070
ISMN 979-0-001-20162-9

Ausgabe mit CD / Edition with CD:
ED 20881
ISMN 979-0-001-17250-9

www.schott-music.com

SCHOTT

Mainz · London · Berlin · Madrid · New York · Paris · Prague · Tokyo · Toronto
© 2015 SCHOTT MUSIC GmbH & Co. KG, Mainz · Printed in Germany

Impressum:

Bestellnummer: ED 22070
ISMN 979-0-001-20162-9
ISBN 978-3-7957-4959-0
Coverfoto: Peter Weilacher. Mit freundlicher Genehmigung von
Paganino – Das Versandhaus für Streichinstrumente und Zubehör
Foto Rückseite: Katharina Deserno (Ezgi, 8 Jahre alt)
BSS 56632 · Printed in Germany

Inhalt / Contents

Vorwort

Das vorliegende Heft enthält eine Auswahl an leichten Stücken für Cello und Klavier, die nach ein bis drei Jahren Cellounterricht spielbar sind. Alle Stücke sind in der 1. Lage ausführbar. Da nur Vortragsstücke, keine Übungstücke ausgewählt wurden, können fortgeschrittene Spielerinnen und Spieler, die das Lagenspiel bereits beherrschen, die Stücke auch auf verschiedenen Lernniveaus musizieren.

Es sind Originalstücke von der Renaissance bis heute enthalten – vom Menuett und der klassischen Sonatine über zeitgenössische Klänge bis hin zu Tango und Pop. Die Stücke sind für den Einzel-, Gruppen- und Kammermusikunterricht geeignet, zum selbstständigen Üben und vor allem für die ersten Vorspiele, Konzerte oder Wettbewerbe.

Lehrerinnen und Lehrer finden im Anhang Kommentare zu den Schwierigkeitsgraden der Stücke sowie einige Unterrichtsideen. Die Epochen sowie die Komponistinnen und Komponisten werden kurz vorgestellt, damit sich Spielerinnen und Spieler ein Bild machen können, aus welcher Zeit die Musik stammt. Ausführlichere Informationen zu den Epochen gibt es im Internet unter www.schott-music.com, Bestellnummer ED 20881, Rubrik "Downloads."
Dieses Heft ist auch als Ausgabe mit CD erschienen (ED 20881). Die CD-Aufnahme soll als Orientierung dienen und das Erlernen der Stücke erleichtern – denn was man schon im Ohr hat, ist viel schneller auch in den Fingern.

Herzlich danken möchte ich Elmar Preusser für seine Unterstützung bei der ersten Vorauswahl der Stücke, Maria Kliegel und Gerhard Mantel für ihre hilfreichen Anregungen sowie Nenad Lečić und Dr. Rainer Mohrs (Schott) für die produktive Zusammenarbeit.
Nun kann die musikalische Reise durch 500 Jahre leichte Cellomusik beginnen – viel Freude und Erfolg dabei wünsche ich allen kleinen und großen Cellistinnen und Cellisten!

Epochen der Musikgeschichte

Renaissance: ab ca. 1430–1600. „Renaissance" bedeutet „Wiedergeburt", d.h. man begeisterte sich für die Ideen der griechischen Antike. In dieser Zeit entwickelte sich die mehrstimmige Musik, der Buchdruck / Notendruck und die Uhr wurden erfunden, Kolumbus entdeckte Amerika, Martin Luther reformierte die Kirche, Leonardo da Vinci malte die *Mona Lisa*.

Barock: ab ca. 1600. In dieser Zeit schrieb Johann Sebastian Bach die *Sechs Suiten* für Cello solo. Antonio Vivaldi schrieb die *Vier Jahreszeiten* und Georg Friedrich Händel das Oratorium *Messias*. Zeit des Absolutismus, der Herrschaft von Adel und Kirche. Das Schloss *Versailles* in Paris stammt aus dieser Zeit sowie z.B. die Gemälde von Rubens, Rembrandt und Caravaggio.

Klassik: von ca. 1770–1826. Wolfgang Amadeus Mozart schrieb die *Zauberflöte*; Ludwig van Beethoven und Joseph Haydn Sonaten und Sinfonien – und vieles mehr. Die Französische Revolution forderte Freiheit, Gleichheit und Brüderlichkeit für alle Menschen und lehnte sich gegen die absolutistischen Herrscher auf. Auch die Musik sollte für alle Menschen verständlich sein. Zur gleichen Zeit lebten und schrieben Johann Wolfgang von Goethe und Friedrich Schiller.

Romantik: ab ca. 1800. Der Begriff kommt von „romanhaft" – in der Romantik standen der Ausdruck von Gefühlen und die Idee einer schöneren, idealen Welt, die es nur in der Kunst gibt, im Vordergrund. Eine Zeit der Gegensätze in Politik, Kunst und Musik.

Musik im 20. und 21. Jahrhundert: In dieser Epoche entstanden viele verschiedene musikalische Stilrichtungen: von klassischer Moderne, Zwölftonmusik über avantgardistische Musik, die mit Geräuschen und experimentellen Techniken arbeitet, bis zu Jazz, Tango, Pop- und Rockmusik.

Katharina Deserno

Preface

This book contains a selection of easy pieces for cello and piano, for students who have had one to three years of cello tuition. All the pieces can be played in first position. These are not exercises but performance pieces, so more advanced players who can already play in higher positions may well enjoy playing them, too.

Original pieces from the Renaissance to the present day are included – from the minuet and the classical sonatina to contemporary sounds, including tango and pop. The pieces are suitable for use in individual or group lessons or in teaching chamber ensembles; they can be learned though individual practice and are suitable for public performance, concerts or competitions.

Teachers will find comments on levels of difficulty in the pieces in the appendix, with some ideas for lessons. A brief introduction to the musical eras and composers gives young players some idea of the historical origins of these pieces. More detailed information on the epochs is available on the Internet at www.schott-music.com, order number ED 20881; 'Downloads'.
This book is also available with CD (ED 20881). The CD recording is meant to help students with learning the pieces – once the sounds are familiar, learning to play the notes becomes much easier.

Heartfelt thanks go to Elmar Preusser for his help with the preliminary selection of pieces, to Maria Kliegel and Gerhard Mantel for their helpful suggestions and to Nenad Lečić and Dr. Rainer Mohrs (Schott) for their constructive collaboration.
Now we can embark on a musical journey through five hundred years of easy cello music – I hope that cellists young and old will enjoy these pieces!

Musical Eras

Renaissance: c. 1430–1600. 'Renaissance' means 'rebirth', expressing a widespread enthusiasm for the ideas of classical Greece. This age saw the emergence of polyphonic music, the printing of books and the invention of the clock; Columbus discovered America, Martin Luther reformed the church and Leonardo da Vinci painted the *Mona Lisa*.

Baroque: from about 1600 onwards. This was the time when Johann Sebastian Bach wrote his *Six Suites* for solo cello. Antonio Vivialdi wrote the *Four Seasons* and George Frederick Handel composed his oratorio *Messiah*. It was an age of absolutism, under the rule of the nobility and the Church. The palace of Versailles in Paris dates from this period, as do the paintings of Rubens, Rembrandt and Caravaggio.

Classical: c. 1770–1826. Wolfgang Amadeus Mozart wrote *The Magic Flute*, Ludwig van Beethoven and Joseph Haydn wrote sonatas and symphonies – and more besides. The French Revolution called for freedom, equality and brotherhood among all mankind, with rebellion against absolute rulers. Music, too, was to be accessible to all. Johann Wolfgang von Goethe and Friedrich Schiller also lived and wrote during this period.

Romantic: from about 1800. The concept of Romanticism emerged with a focus on the expression of feelings and the idea of a more beautiful, idealised world only to be found in art. This was an age of extremes in politics, art and music.

Music of the 20th and 21st Centuries: this era has seen the emergence of many different musical styles, from classical modernism, twelve tone music and *avant garde* music, working with noises and experimental techniques, through to jazz, tango, pop and rock music.

Katharina Deserno
Translation Julia Rushworth

Über die Komponisten

Milán, Luis (um 1500 – nach 1560): spanischer Musiker, Schriftsteller, Komponist, Autor der ersten gedruckten Musik für Vihuela (ein spanisches Saiteninstrument aus dem 16. Jh., vom Bau her der Laute und Gambe verwandt). Die Saiten wurden entweder wie bei der Gitarre gezupft oder mit einem Bogen wie beim Cello gestrichen.
Die *Pavane* ist ein feierlicher Schreittanz aus Italien, der an den Königshöfen in ganz Europa getanzt wurde. Milán war einer der ersten Komponisten, die Pavanen schrieben und die ihre Musik mit Tempo-Angaben versahen.

Willem De Fesch (1687–1761): niederländischer Komponist und Geiger. De Fesch war in Amsterdam, Antwerpen und London tätig. Er war Konzertmeister in einem von Georg Friedrich Händel geleiteten Orchester, schrieb Oratorien, Messen, Konzerte, Duette, Sonaten und Lieder. *Arietta* bedeutet soviel wie „kleine Arie" oder „Liedchen".

Giambattista Cirri (1724–1808): italienischer Komponist und Cellist, er spielte als Solocellist am Theater in Neapel und auch einmal in einem Konzert in London gemeinsam mit Mozart, der damals gerade 8 Jahre alt war. Seine Kompositionen trugen dazu bei, dass das Cello als Melodieinstrument und nicht nur als Begleitinstrument beliebt wurde.

Christoph Schaffrath (1709–1763): deutscher Cembalist, Komponist und Lehrer. 1733 bewarb sich Schaffrath um eine Stelle als Organist an der Sophienkirche in Dresden, die aber Wilhelm Friedemann Bach, der Sohn Johann Sebastian Bachs, bekam. Im Dienst von Kronprinz Friedrich und seiner Schwester Prinzessin Amalia komponierte er Kammermusik- und Orchesterwerke, vor allem aber Musik für Klavier bzw. Cembalo solo oder für Cembalo mit einem Melodieinstrument.

Stephen Paxton, (1734–1787): englischer Cellist. Er schrieb zahlreiche Werke für sein Instrument, das Cello: Konzerte, Solostücke und Duette, aber auch Messen und Chorwerke.

Joseph Reinagle (1762–1825): englischer Musiker. Reinagle war nicht nur professioneller Cellist, sondern auch als Hornist, Trompeter, Geiger, Bratschist, Orchesterleiter und Komponist tätig – ein Multitalent! Er führte als Cellist die Cellokonzerte von Joseph Haydn auf, den er bewunderte und an dessen Musik er sich in seinen Werken orientierte. Er schrieb verschiedene Duette und Celloschulen.

Alexander Tichonowitsch Gretchaninoff (1864–1956): russisch-amerikanischer Komponist. Er schrieb Opern, Sinfonien, Kammermusik, ein Cellokonzert, Lieder und viele Werke für Kinder, z.B. Kinderopern, Liedersammlungen, Klavierstücke und die Sammlung *In aller Frühe* für Cello und Klavier. Er engagierte sich politisch und sozial, arbeitete mit Kinderchören, organisierte Gesangsprojekte für obdachlose Kinder, Gesprächskonzerte für Arbeiter, er schrieb eine „Hymne auf ein freies Russland", baute das Moskauer Puppentheater wieder mit auf und war Mitglied in Jurys bei Kinder-Kompositionswettbewerben.

Hugo Schlemüller (1872–1918): war als Cellist in München und Leipzig tätig und unterrichtete am Konservatorium in Frankfurt. Er schrieb ein Violoncello-Konzert sowie zahlreiche andere Stücke für Cello von leicht bis schwer.

Paul Hindemith (1895–1963): deutscher Komponist, Bratschist und Geiger. 1927 wurde Hindemith Professor für Komposition an der Berliner Musikhochschule, er galt zu dieser Zeit als einer der bedeutendsten deutschen Komponisten. 1933 wurde seine Musik von den Nationalsozialisten verboten. Hindemith ging in dieser Zeit in die Türkei, auf Einladung der türkischen Regierung, um dort am Aufbau des Musiklebens nach mitteleuropäischen Maßstäben mitzuarbeiten. Es gelang ihm, einige jüdische Musiker, die von den Nazis verfolgt wurden, in die Türkei zu holen. Ab 1940 unterrichtete er an der School of Music der Yale University. Seit den 1950er Jahren war Hindemith in der ganzen Welt als Dirigent unterwegs. Er hat ein umfangreiches Werk hinterlassen: Opern, Kammermusik, Lieder, Chöre, Orchesterwerke, Filmmusik, Unterrichtswerke, theoretische Bücher und vieles mehr. Die *Drei kleinen Stücke* für Cello und Klavier schrieb Hindemith für seine Frau Gertrud, die ausgebildete Sängerin war und als Hobby zu Hause Cello spielte.

Bruno Stürmer (1892–1958): deutscher Dirigent, Komponist, Lehrer, Musikkritiker, Opern- und Chordirigent sowie Musikschulleiter. Stürmer komponierte in einem melodischen, neo-klassizistischen Stil, sein *Allegretto* erinnert ein wenig an ein Menuett. Er lebte zur gleichen Zeit wie Paul Hindemith. Seine Musik wurde jedoch nicht verboten, er komponierte sogar Stücke für die Festtage der Nationalsozialisten.

Hermann Regner (1928–2008): Komponist und Musikpädagoge, war Schüler von Carl Orff und Professor für Musiktheorie und Komposition in Salzburg. Er stellte sein Leben und Wirken unter das Motto „Musik lieben lernen" und hielt Vorträge in der ganzen Welt, setzte sich besonders für musikalische Früherziehung ein und komponierte Stücke für Kinder und Jugendliche.

Barbara Heller (*1936): Komponistin, Pianistin und Musikwissenschaftlerin, komponierte Werke für verschiedene Instrumente, Kammermusik, Orchesterwerke, Filmmusik sowie elektroakustische Musik und Klanginstallationen. In dem Stück *Lalai* verwendet sie ein iranisches Lied mit dem gleichen Titel. Es ist 50 iranischen Frauen gewidmet, die 1989 im Evin-Gefängnis in Teheran umgebracht wurden.

Frank Wunsch (*1945): Jazzpianist und Komponist, studierte Klavier und Komposition in Dortmund und Köln. Sine internationale Konzerttätigkeit und zahlreiche CD- und Rundfunkaufnahmen dokumentieren das Schaffen von Frank Wunsch. Seit 1980 unterrichtet er an der Musikhochschule in Köln und wurde 2003 zum Professor ernannt. Neben zahlreichen Stücken für Klavier und verschiedene kleine Besetzungen komponiert er auch Stücke für Big Band und großes Orchester.

Gabriel Koeppen (*1958): Cellist, Saxophonist, Komponist, Dozent an der Universität Flensburg sowie Leiter der Musikschule in Flensburg. Er komponiert zahlreiche Stücke für Cello von ganz leicht bis sehr anspruchsvoll – Blues, Pop, Tango, Rock'n Roll und vieles mehr.

Daniel Kemminer (*1978): Musikstudium an der Kölner Musikhochschule, als Sänger Mitwirkung in verschiedenen Opernproduktionen, Gründungsmitglied der Ensembles *Garage* und *Groba* für Neue Musik. Kemminer arbeitet als Musiklehrer am Gymnasium; als Pianist ist er tätig im Kabarett- und Pop-Bereich. Er schrieb zahlreiche Arrangements und Kompositionen für Gesangsensemble und verschiedene Instrumentalbesetzungen.

Eduard Pütz (1911–2000) studierte Schulmusik und Mathematik in Köln, war Lehrer am Gymnasium in Rheinbach sowie Dozent für Komposition und Musiktheorie an der Rheinischen Musikschule in Köln. Er komponierte zahlreiche Werke, darunter eine Oper, Orchesterwerke, Kammermusik, Pop-und Jazzstücke. In seiner Musik wollte er Brücken zwischen der sog. E-Musik und U-Musik bauen, also eine Verbindung zwischen Klassik und Pop/Jazz erreichen.

Quellenangaben (Auswahl)

The New Grove Dictionary of Music and Musicians. Sadie Stanley (Hg.) New York 2001
Musik in Geschichte und Gegenwart. (MGG) Allgemeine Enzyklopädie der Musik begründet von Friedrich Blume. Ludwig Finscher (Hg.) Kassel, Basel, London 1994f.
Lexikon Musik und Gender. Annette Kreutziger-Herr, Melanie Unseld (Hg.) Kassel 2010

Notes on the composers

Milán, Luis (c. 1500 – after 1560): a Spanish musician, writer, composer and author of the first printed music for the vihuela (a sixteenth-century Spanish string instrument, similar to the lute and gamba in construction). The strings were either plucked like a guitar or played with a bow like a cello.
The *Pavane* is a solemn-paced dance from Italy that was danced at royal courts all over Europe. Milán was one of the first composers to write pavanes and to put tempo markings in their music.

Willem De Fesch (1687–1761): a Dutch composer and violinist. De Fesch worked in Amsterdam, Antwerp and London. He was leader of an orchestra conducted by George Frederick Handel and wrote oratorios, masses, concertos, duets, sonatas and songs. *Arietta* means 'little aria' or 'little song'.

Giambattista Cirri (1724–1808): an Italian composer and cellist who was principal cellist at the theatre in Naples and once appeared in a concert in London with Mozart, who was just eight years old at the time. His compositions helped to make the cello popular as a melodic instrument, not solely for bass accompaniment.

Christoph Schaffrath (1709–1763): a German harpsichordist, composer and teacher. In 1773 Schaffrath applied for a position as organist at St Sophia's Church in Dresden, but the post went to Wilhelm Friedemann Bach, son of Johann Sebastian Bach. Employed by Crown Prince Friedrich and his sister Princess Amalia, Schaffrath composed chamber ensembles and orchestral works, though most of his music was for keyboard, harpsichord or harpsichord with a melodic instrument.

Stephen Paxton (1734–1787): an English cellist. He wrote numerous works for his instrument, the cello – concertos, solo pieces and duets – as well as masses and choral works.

Joseph Reinagle (1762–1825): an English musician. Reinagle was not only a professional cellist, but also played the horn, trumpet, violin and viola; he was also an orchestral conductor and composer – a man of many talents! As a cellist he performed the cello concertos of Joseph Haydn, whom he admired and whose music provided inspiration for Reinagle's own compositions. He wrote various duets and cello tutorial books.

Alexander Tikhonovich Gretchaninov (1864–1956): a Russian-American composer who wrote operas, symphonies, chamber music, a cello concerto, songs and numerous works for children, including children's operas, collections of songs, piano pieces and the collection *Early in the morning* for cello and piano. He involved himself in politics and community projects, working with children's choirs, organising singing workshops for homeless children and concerts for working people with spoken introductions to the pieces. He wrote a 'Hymn for a free Russia', helped to re-establish the Moscow puppet theatre and served as an adjudicator for children's composition competitions.

Hugo Schlemüller (1872–1918): cellist and cello teacher. He lived in Munich, Leipzig and Frankfurt where he taught at the Conservatoire. He wrote a cello concerto and numerous other pieces for the cello, ranging from easy to difficult.

Paul Hindemith (1895–1963): a German composer, viola player and violinist. Hindemith was appointed professor of composition at the Academy of Music in Berlin in 1927, when he ranked as one of the most important composers in Germany. In 1933 the Nazis banned his music and Hindemith then went to Turkey, invited by the turkish government to work in musical education there. He managed to get Jewish musicians who were persecuted by the Nazis to move to Turkey. From 1940 onwards he taught at the School of Music at Yale University. From the 1950s onwards Hindemith travelled all over the world as a conductor. His many compositions include operas, chamber music, songs, choral pieces, orchestral works, film music, tutorial works, books on music theory and more besides. Hindemith's *Three Little Pieces* for cello and piano were written for his wife Gertrud, a trained singer who enjoyed playing the cello at home.

Bruno Stürmer (1892–1958): a German conductor, composer, teacher, music critic, operatic and choral conductor and music school director. Stürmer composed in a melodic, neoclassical style: his *Allegretto* is rather like a minuet. A contemporary of Paul Hindemith, Stürmer's music was not banned: he even wrote pieces for Nazi festivals.

Hermann Regner (1928–2008): a composer engaged in musical education, Regner was a student of Carl Orff and went on to be a professor of music theory and composition in Salzburg. 'Learning to love music' became the motto for his life's work as he gave lectures all over the world, placed particular emphasis on early musical education and composed pieces for children and young people.

Barbara Heller (b. 1936): a composer, pianist and musicologist who has composed pieces for various instruments, chamber ensembles, orchestral works, film music, electro-acoustic pieces and sound installations. *Lalai* is a setting of an Iranian song with the same title: it is dedicated to fifty Iranian women who were murdered in Evin prison in Teheran in 1989.

Frank Wunsch (b. 1945) is a jazz pianist and composer. He studied the piano and composition in Dortmund and Cologne; international concert tours and numerous CD and radio recordings document his subsequent creative work. Since 1980 Frank Wunsch has taught at the Academy of Music in Cologne, where he was appointed Professor in 2003. Besides numerous pieces for the piano and various small ensembles he has also composed pieces for Big Band and large orchestra.

Gabriel Koeppen (b. 1958): a cellist, saxophonist, composer, lecturer at the University of Flensburg and director of the Flensburg Academy of Music. He has composed numerous pieces for the cello, ranging from very easy to technically challenging music – blues, pop, tango, rock'n'roll and more besides.

Daniel Kemminer (b. 1978): studied music at Musikhochschule Köln (Cologne Academy of Music). As a singer he has been involved in various operatic productions and is a founding member of contemporary music ensembles *Garage* and *Groba*. Kemminer is a secondary school music teacher and plays piano in cabaret and pop events. He has written numerous arrangements and compositions for vocal ensemble and various combinations of instruments.

Eduard Pütz (1911–2000) studied music teaching and mathematics in Cologne, taught at a secondary school in Rheinbach and lectured in composition and music theory at the Rheinische Musikschule (Rhein Music Academy) in Cologne. He composed numerous works including an opera, symphonic works, chamber music, pop and jazz pieces. With his music he wanted to build bridges between 'serious' music and the world of entertainment, forging a link between classical traditions and pop and jazz music.

Sources (selected)

The New Grove Dictionary of Music and Musicians. Sadie Stanley (ed.) New York 2001
Musik in Geschichte und Gegenwart. (MGG) A general encyclopaedia of music founded by Friedrich Blume. Ludwig Finscher (ed.) Kassel, Basel, London 1994f.
Lexikon Musik und Gender. Annette Kreutziger-Herr, Melanie Unseld (ed.) Kassel 2010

I. Renaissance
Pavane

Don Luis Milán
(ca 1500–1560)

II. Barock / Baroque

Arietta

Willem de Fesch
(1687–1761)
(Basso continuo: Hugo Ruf)

aus / from: W. de Fesch, Sonate d-Moll / D minor op. 8/3, Schott CB 54

Menuetto

Giambattista Cirri
(1724–1808)

3

aus / from: G. Cirri, Sonate No. 3

14

Allegro

Christoph Schaffrath
(ca. 1709–1763)
(Basso continuo: Hugo Ruf)

aus / from: C. Schaffrath, Sonate G-Dur / G major, Schott CB 157

III. Klassik / Classical Age

Sonate

Stephen Paxton
(1735–1787)
(Basso continuo: Freda Dinn)

aus /from: St. Paxton, Sonate D-Dur / D major op. 3/2, Schott ED 11057 (1. Satz / 1st movement)

Sonatine G-Dur / G major

I

Joseph Reinagle
(1762–1836)
(Klavierbegleitung: Jens Schlichting)

*) Original:

Einzelausgabe / Single Edition: J. Reinagle, Sonatine, Schott CB 223

*) Original:

22

II

24

III

Presto ♩. = ca 80 - 88

IV. Romantik / Romantic Age
Morgenspaziergang / Morning Stroll

Alexander Gretchaninoff
(1864–1956)

aus / from: A Gretchaninoff, In aller Frühe / Early Morning, op. 126 a, Schott ED 2143

In der Dämmerung / Twilight

Alexander Gretchaninoff
(1864–1956)

10

aus / from: A Gretchaninoff, In aller Frühe / Early Morning, op. 126 a, Schott ED 2143

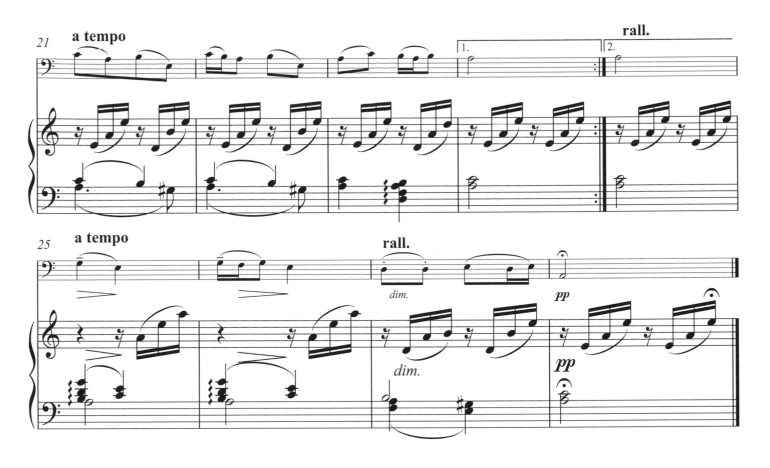

Am Winterabend / On Winter's Eve

Alexander Gretchaninoff
(1864–1956)

aus / from: A Gretchaninoff, In aller Frühe / Early Morning, op. 126 a, Schott ED 2143

Scherzo

Hugo Schlemüller
(1872–1918)

aus / from: H. Schlemüller, 6 leichte Vortragsstücke / 6 easy concert pieces op. 12

Ländler

Hugo Schlemüller
(1872–1918)

aus / from: H. Schlemüller, 6 leichte Vortragsstücke / 6 easy concert pieces op. 12

Katharina Deserno

Mein erstes Konzert

My First Concert

25 leichte Vortragsstücke aus 5 Jahrhunderten
25 Easy Concert Pieces from 5 Centuries

für Violoncello und Klavier
for Violoncello and Piano

ED 22070
ISMN 979-0-001-20162-9

Ausgabe mit CD / Edition with CD:
ED 20881
ISMN 979-0-001-17250-9

Violoncello

www.schott-music.com

Mainz · London · Berlin · Madrid · New York · Paris · Prague · Tokyo · Toronto
© 2015 SCHOTT MUSIC GmbH & Co. KG, Mainz · Printed in Germany

Inhalt / Contents

I. Renaissance
Pavane

Don Luis Milán
(ca. 1500–1560)

II. Barock / Baroque
Arietta

Larghetto e piano ♪ ca. 72 - 80

Willem de Fesch
(1687 - 1761)

2

aus / from: W. de Fesch, Sonate d-Moll / D minor op. 8/3, Schott CB 54

*) ossia:

Menuetto

Giambattista Cirri
(1724–1808)

3

aus / from: G. Cirri, Sonate Nr. 3

Allegro

Christoph Schaffrath
(ca. 1709–1763)

*) [musical note figure]

aus / from: C. Schaffrath, Sonate G-Dur / G major, Schott CB 157

6

*) Bogen bei punktierten Noten an den Frosch zurückholen / take bow back to frog:

Fr.

III. Klassik / Classical Age
Sonate

Stephen Paxton
(1735–1787)

Allegretto ♩ ca. 88

*) Original:

aus / from: St. Paxton, Sonate D-Dur / D major op. 3/2, Schott ED 11057 (1. Satz / 1st movement)

Sonatine G-Dur / G major

I

Joseph Reinagle
(1762–1836)

*) Original:

Einzelausgabe / Single edition: J. Reinagle, Sonatine, Schott CB 223

II

Andante ♩ ca. 84

7

III

Presto ♩. ca. 80 - 88

8

IV. Romantik / Romantic Age
Morgenspaziergang / Morning Stroll

Alexander Gretchaninoff
(1864–1956)

aus / from: A. Gretchaninoff, In aller Frühe / Early Morning, op. 126b, Schott ED 2143

In der Dämmerung / Twilight

Alexander Gretchaninoff
(1864–1956)

aus / from: A. Gretchaninoff, In aller Frühe / Early Morning, op. 126b, Schott ED 2143

Am Winterabend / On Winter's Eve

Alexander Gretchaninoff
(1864–1956)

aus /from: A. Gretchaninoff, In aller Frühe / Early Morning op. 126b, Schott ED 2143

Scherzo

Hugo Schlemüller
(1872–1918)

aus / from: H. Schlemüller, 6 leichte Vortragsstücke / 6 easy concert pieces op. 12

Ländler

Hugo Schlemüller
(1872–1918)

*) ossia:

aus / from: H. Schlemüller, 6 leichte Vortragsstücke / 6 easy concert pieces op. 12

V. Moderne / Zeitgenössische Epoche
Modern Age (20th/21th Century)
Kleine Hausmusik

Bruno Stürmer
(1892–1958)

aus / from: B. Stürmer, Kleine Hausmusik / Little House Music No. 3, Schott ED 2685

Leichtes Stück / Easy Piece

Paul Hindemith
(1895–1963)

aus / from: P. Hindemith, Drei leichte Stücke / Three easy pieces, Schott ED 2771 (No. 1)

Lalai
Schlaflied zum Wachwerden?
A Lullaby to awaken you?

Barbara Heller
(* 1936)

aus / from: B. Heller, Lalai, Schlaflied zum Wachwerden, Schott CB 155

Von einem anderen Stern / From Another Planet

Hermann Regner
(1928–2008)

Weil die Musik „von einem anderen Stern" ganz anders klingt, spielt der Cellist Flageolett-Töne. Sie sind hier so notiert wie sie klingen. Wenn die Noten eng beieinander stehen, folgen sie schnell aufeinander; sind sie weiter voneinander entfernt notiert, kommen sie langsamer nacheinander. (H. Regner)

The "Music from Another Planet" sounds quite different. Here the Cellist plays harmonics. They are notated where they sound. If the notes are close to each other they follow quickly one after the other; if they are further apart they follow each other more slowly. (H. Regner)

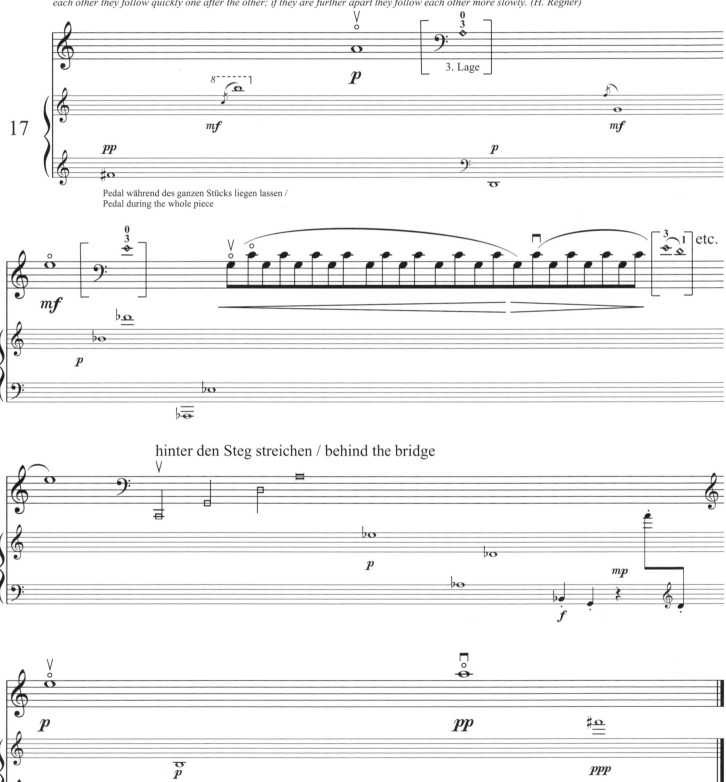

Pedal während des ganzen Stücks liegen lassen /
Pedal during the whole piece

hinter den Steg streichen / behind the bridge

aus / from: H. Regner, Mein Lieblingslied von gestern / My favourite Song from yesterday (No.6), Schott ED 8194

VI. Rock, Pop, Tango und mehr / Rock, Pop, Tango and more

Spiritual

Eduard Pütz
(1911–2000)

aus / from: E. Pütz, Short Stories, 10 Easy Pieces for Cello and Piano, Schott ED 7533

Dorian Blue

Frank Wunsch
(*1945)

aus / from: F. Wunsch, Blues for two (Klavier vierhändig / Piano Duet), Schott ED 20189
für Cello und Klavier bearbeitet / arranged for Cello and Piano by K. Deserno

Windlied / Wind Song

Gabriel Koeppen
(*1958)

Percussion-Ensemble

Hi-Hat:
Fingernagel auf Korpus/Stimme: „ts-ts"

Snare: Schlag auf Zarge/Stimme: „ka"

Bass-Drums:
Hand o. Faust auf Korpus/Stimme: „dum"

Disco Hit

Gabriel Koeppen
(*1958)

1) „Bass-Drum": Der Cellist schlägt mit der linken flachen Hand auf die Decke.
Der Pianist klatsch oder schlägt auf einem bassig klingenden Teil des Klavieres, z.B. von unten gegen den Tastenkasten.

2) Cellist: Glissando in beliebiger Tonhöhe und/oder hoher Ruf auf „Huh".

Percussion-Ensemble (ad lib.)

Hi-Hat/Shaker/Stimme „zick-e-zick-e"

Snare/Schlag auf Zarge/Stimme „ka"

Bass-Drums/flache Hand o. Faust
auf Korpus/Stimme „dum"

Am Strand / At the Beach

Gabriel Koeppen
(*1958)

Percussion-Ensemble

Shaker/Reiben/Stimme „zick-e-zick-e"

Click: Bogenstange auf Zargenrand/Claves/Stimme „ka"

Bass-Drum: Hand o. Faust auf Korpus/Tiefe Stimme „dum"

Lords of Chords
(Metal Cello-Rock)

Daniel Kemminer
(*1978)

Los niños del Tango

Daniel Kemminer
(*1978)

Shana Tova / Gutes neues Jahr / Happy New Year

(Klezmer)

Daniel Kemminer
(*1978)

V. Moderne / Zeitgenössische Epoche
Modern Age (20th/21th Century)
Kleine Hausmusik

Bruno Stürmer
(1892–1958)

aus / from: B. Stürmer, Kleine Hausmusik / Little House Music No. 3, Schott ED 2685

Leichtes Stück / Easy Piece

Paul Hindemith
(1895–1963)

Mäßig schnell, munter ♩ ca. 92

15

aus / from: P. Hindemith, Drei leichte Stücke / Three easy pieces, Schott ED 2771 (No. 1)

Lalai
Schlaflied zum Wachwerden?
A Lullaby to awaken you?

Barbara Heller
(* 1936)
(Bearbeitung der Cellostimme: K. Deserno)

Thema
Ruhig ♩ ca. 92

aus / from B. Heller, Lalai, Schaflied zum Wachwerden, Schott CB 155

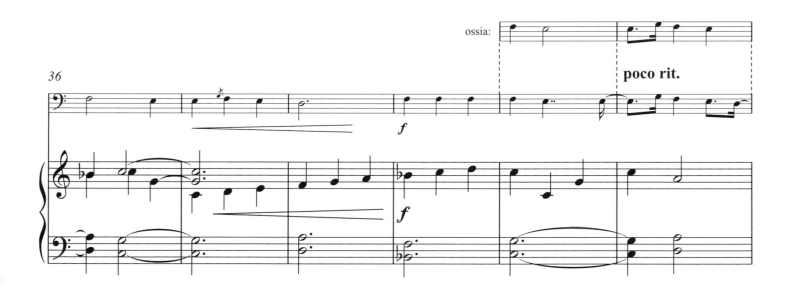

Von einem anderen Stern / From Another Planet

Hermann Regner
(1928–2008)

Weil die Musik "von einem anderen Stern" ganz anders klingt, spielt der Cellist Flageolett-Töne. Sie sind hier so notiert wie sie klingen. Wenn die Noten eng beieinander stehen, folgen sie schnell aufeinander; sind sie weiter voneinander entfernt notiert, kommen sie langsamer nacheinander. (H. Regner)

The "Music from Another Planet" sounds quite different. Here the Cellist plays harmonics. They are notated where they sound. If the notes are close to each other they follow quickly one after the other; if they are further apart they follow each other more slowly. (H. Regner)

aus / from: H. Regner, Mein Lieblingslied von gestern / My favourite Song from yesterday (No. 6), Schott ED 8194

VI. Rock, Pop, Tango und mehr / Rock, Pop, Tango and more

Spiritual

Eduard Pütz
(1911–2000)

aus / from: E. Pütz, Short Stories, 10 Easy Pieces for Cello and Piano, Schott ED 7533

Dorian Blue

Frank Wunsch
(*1945)

aus / from: F. Wunsch, Blues for two (Klavier vierhändig / Piano Duet), Schott ED 20189
für Cello und Klavier bearbeitet / arranged for Cello and Piano by K. Deserno

Aus wendetechnischen Gründen bleibt diese Seite frei.
This page is left blank to save an unnecessary page turn.
On laisse une page blanche pour faciliter la tourne.

Windlied / Wind Song

Gabriel Koeppen
(*1958)

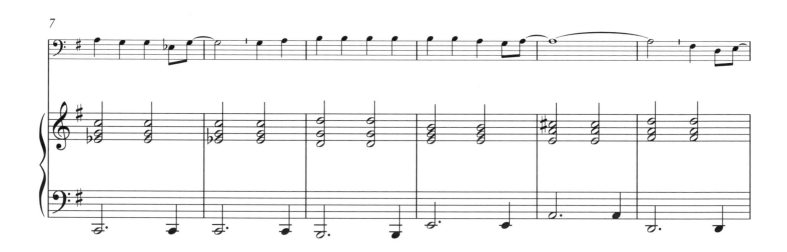

*) r. H. beim ersten Mal eine Oktave tiefer spielen
r. h. one octave lower at the first time

18

23

28

Percussion-Ensemble

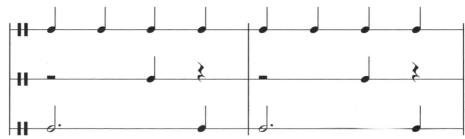

Hi-Hat:
Fingernagel auf Korpus/Stimme: „ts-ts"

Snare: Schlag auf Zarge/Stimme: „ka"

Bass-Drum:
Hand o. Faust auf Korpus/Stimme: „dum"

Disco Hit

Gabriel Koeppen
(*1958)

1) „Bassdrum": Der Cellist schlägt mit der linken flachen Hand auf die Decke.
   Der Pianist klatscht oder schlägt auf einem bassig klingenden Teil des Klavieres,
   z.B. von unten gegen den Tastenkasten.

2) Cellist: Glissando in beliebiger Tonhöhe und/oder hoher Ruf auf „Huh".
   Pianist: Klatschen und/oder hoher Ruf auf „Huh".

Percussion-Ensemble (ad lib.)

Hi-Hat/Shaker/Stimme „zick-e-zick-e"

Snare/Schlag auf Zarge/Stimme „ka"

Bass-Drum/flache Hand o. Faust auf Korpus/Stimme „dum"

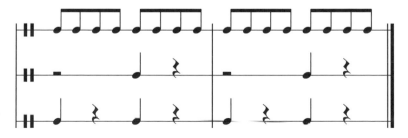

Am Strand / At the Beach

Gabriel Koeppen
(*1958)

dal 𝄉 al ⊕
poi al coda

Percussion-Ensemble

Shaker/Reiben/Stimme „zick-e-zick-e"

Click: Bogenstange auf Zargenrand/Claves/Stimme „ka"

Bassdrum: Hand o. Faust auf Korpus/tiefe Stimme „dum"

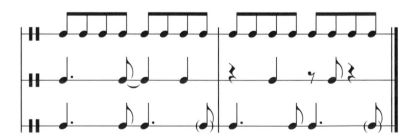

Aus wendetechnischen Gründen bleibt diese Seite frei.
This page is left blank to save an unnecessary page turn.
On laisse une page blanche pour faciliter la tourne.

Lords of Chords
(Metal-Cello-Rock)

Daniel Kemminer
(*1978)

*) 𝄐 ad lib.

Los niños del Tango

Daniel Kemminer
(*1978)

Tempo di Tango ♩ ca. 116

Shana Tova / Gutes neues Jahr / Happy New Year
(Klezmer)

Daniel Kemminer
(*1978)

Hinweise für den Unterricht

1. Milán, *Pavane*: 1. Lage, enger Griff; Bogeneinteilung „Wanderstrich", Echodynamik, die Bassstimme des Klaviers kann als „Basso continuo" von Lehrerin, Lehrer oder anderen Schülern mitgespielt werden, wie es im Barock üblich war.

2. de Fesch, *Arietta*: 1. Lage, enger und weiter Griff nach unten, barocke Phrasierung, schwer/leicht, zurückgeholter Abstrich, unausgeglichene Bogeneinteilung; die Bassstimme des Klaviers kann als „Basso continuo" mitgespielt werden.

3. Cirri, *Menuetto*: 1. Lage enger und weiter Griff nach unten, Betonung auf eins, zweitaktige Phrasierung, Verzierungen; die Bassstimme des Klaviers kann als „Basso continuo" mitgespielt werden.

4. Schaffrath, *Allegro*: 1. Lage, enger Griff, einmal weiter Griff nach oben, kurze, federnde Achtel, Sechzehntelnoten an der Saite, Echo-Dynamik, Geläufigkeit links, Koordination rechts; die Bassstimme des Klaviers kann als „Basso continuo" mitgespielt werden.

5. Paxton, *Allegretto*: 1. Lage, enger und weiter Griff nach oben, Vorschläge, Triller, klassische Phrasierung, schwer/leicht; die Bassstimme des Klaviers kann als „Basso continuo" mitgespielt werden.

6. Reinagle, *Sonatine*, 1. Satz: 1. Lage enger und weiter Griff nach oben, Bogentechnik, Bogeneinteilung, Dynamik; die Bassstimme des Klaviers ist in der ganzen Sonatine auch als zweite Cellostimme spielbar. Es existiert eine Originalfassung von J. Reinagle als Duo für zwei Violoncelli in „Progressive Lessons for the Violoncello".

7. Reinagle, *Sonatine*, 2. Satz: 1. Lage, enger und weiter Griff nach oben, langsame Bogengeschwindigkeit auf gesungenen Tönen, schwer/leicht Phrasierung, Vibrato

8. Reinagle, *Sonatine*, 3. Satz: 1. Lage, enger Griff, Triolen, unregelmäßige Bogeneinteilung (zwei Triolenachtel im Abstrich gebunden, eines im Aufstrich leicht zurück), Koordination.

9. Gretchaninoff, *Morgenspaziergang*: 1. Lage enger Griff, Linien, Kammermusikspiel, einfaches pizzicato, es wird der Wechsel zwischen arco und pizzicato gelernt, am besten mit dem Zeigefinger zupfen.

10. Gretchaninoff, *In der Dämmerung*: 1. Lage enger Griff, legato, Saitenübergänge, (Vibrato).

11. Gretchaninoff, Am Winterabend: 1. Lage, enger und weiter Griff, ½ Lage, Wechsel zwischen erster und halber Lage, Fingerwechsel auf dem gleichen Ton.

12. Schlemüller, *Scherzo* op.12/3: 1. Lage, enger Griff, Bogentechnik, Saitenübergänge, wenig Bogen benutzen, kurze Staccato-Achtel, Klang auf langen Noten, Charakterwechsel im Mittelteil, legato.

13. Schlemüller, *Ländler* op. 12/4: 1. Lage, enger Griff, Bogeneinteilung, legato, Schwung auf Eins.

14. Stürmer, *Allegro giocoso*: 1. Lage, enger und weiter Griff nach oben und unten, „klassischer" Charakter mit neuen Harmonien, Stimmungswechsel.

15. Hindemith, *Leichtes Stück*: 1. Lage, enger und weiter Griff nach oben und unten, einmal halbe Lage, Kammermusikspiel, Dialoge, Charakterwechsel.

16. Heller, *Lalai*: 1. Lage, enger und weiter Griff nach unten, rhythmische Variationen als notiertes Rubato, gesungene Linien, Dynamik, mit Klangfarben experimentieren, z.B.: *Forte* mit langsamer Bogengeschwindigkeit näher am Steg, piano mit „hauchigem" Klang und schneller Bogengeschwindigkeit am Griffbrett, *pianissimo* ganz zurückhaltend „wie mit einem Haar", *morendo*, den Schlusston verklingen lassen.

17. Regner, *Von einem anderen Stern*: erste Begegnung mit Spieltechniken Neuer Musik, Flageoletts in der 3. Lage, 1. Finger liegt dort, wo der 4. in der 1. Lage liegt, 3. darüber. Die Flageoletts können auch in den hohen Lagen ausprobiert und gespielt werden.

18. Pütz, *Spiritual*: 1. Lage, enger Griff, ausgeglichene (z.B. T. 1-8) und unausgeglichene (z.B. T. 11, 12, 13) Bogeneinteilung. Optional kann ab T. 16 auf 4 in der 3. Lage eine Oktave höher weitergespielt werden, der Fingerwechsel auf dem gleichen Ton erleichtert das Experimentieren mit einer neuen Lage.

19. Wunsch, *Dorian Blue*: 1. Lage, enger Griff, swingende Legato-Achtel, „Bluesfeeling", Zusammenspiel.

20. Koeppen, *Windlied*: 1. Lage, enger Griff, einmal weiter Griff nach unten, Bogeneinteilung; ausgeglichene Bogeneinteilung mit Wanderstrich (T. 12, T. 16, T. 24); Bogen zurückholen, dabei lange Note leicht abkürzen (T. 4, T. 8, T. 22, T. 30). Hier kann eine Percussion-Gruppe mitspielen. Im Gruppenunterricht können die SchülerInnen abwechselnd einen oder mehrere notierte Rhythmen auf dem Cello oder mit der Stimme dazu erzeugen, so dass eine eigene „Combo" entsteht. Außerdem kann auch die Bassstimme des Klaviers als weitere Cellostimme verwendet werden, im notierten Rhythmus oder in durchgehenden Vierteln (T. 9, 15, 19, 27 müssen dazu oktaviert werden). Man kann das Stück auch nach Phrasen unterteilt spielen lassen, z.B. wie Frage und Antwort (alle vier Takte wechseln).

21. Koeppen, *Disco-Hit*: 1. Lage, enger und weiter Griff nach oben und unten, Wechsel zwischen weitem Griff nach unten und oben, Rhythmus. Beim Klatschen und Rufen kann variiert werden, das Stück kann auch von vorne und mehrfach wiederholt werden, so dass mehrere Strophen entstehen. Hier kann eine Percussion-Gruppe (siehe *Windlied*) mitspielen. Soll eine größere Gruppe beteiligt werden, könnte eine Choreographie entwickelt werden.

22. Koeppen, *Am Strand*: 1. Lage enger und weiter Griff nach oben und unten, Synkopen, glissando zum Flageolett 5. Lage (optional), Hochschieben des 4. Fingers in den weiten Griff wie ein Lagenwechsel (T. 21, T. 33). Hier kann eine Percussion-Gruppe (siehe *Windlied*) mitspielen.

23. Kemminer, *Lord of Chords*: 1. Lage, enger und weiter Griff nach unten, Quintgriffe, Synkopen, Ausdauer – nicht zu oft hintereinander spielen lassen wegen anstrengender Griffe links und Kraft rechts, damit keine Verkrampfungen entstehen. Hier kann ein Schlagzeug mitspielen, das Stück kann auch mit einer Cellogruppe musiziert werden, es können dann auch die Quintgriffe in zwei Stimmen geteilt werden.

24. Kemminer, *Los niños del Tango*: 1. Lage, enger und weiter Griff nach oben, übermäßiger Griff zwischen 4. und 2. Finger, am besten wie einen Lagenwechsel spielen, glissando in die 4. Lage (T. 25, optional), die daran evtl. zum ersten Mal besprochen und ausprobiert werden kann; Charakter-, Dynamik- und Klangfarbenunterschiede.

25. Kemminer, *Shana Tova*: 1. Lage, enger und weiter Griff nach unten und oben, übermäßiges Intervall, rubato-Zusammenspiel; im Gruppenunterricht können arco- und pizzicato-Abschnitte aufgeteilt werden.

Notes for teaching purposes

1. Milán, *Pavane*: 1st closed position, bowing with a 'wandering stroke', echo dynamics; the bass line of the piano part may be played as *basso continuo* by the teacher or other students, as was customary in the Baroque era.

2. De Fesch, *Arietta*: 1st closed position and stretched 1st finger, baroque phrasing, strong/ weak beats, retaking down-bows, irregular bowing patterns; the bass line of the piano part may be played as a *basso continuo*.

3. Cirri, *Menuetto*: 1st closed position and stretched 1st finger, emphasis on the first beat, two-bar phrasing, ornamentation; the bass line of the piano part may be played as a *basso continuo*.

4. Schaffrath, *Allegro*: 1st position, closed position and once stretched 4th finger, short, bouncy quavers, semiquavers played on the string, echo dynamics, left-hand agility, right-hand coordination; the bass line of the piano part may be played as a *basso continuo*.

5. Paxton, *Allegretto:* 1st position, closed position and stretched 4th finger, grace notes, trills, classical phrasing, strong/weak beats; the bass line of the piano part may be played as a *basso continuo*.

6. Reinagle, *Sonatine*, 1st movement: 1st position, closed position and stretched 4th finger, bowing technique, bow distribution, dynamics; the bass line of the piano part for the whole sonatina may be played as a second cello part. There is an original version by J. Reinagle as a duo for two cellos in 'Progressive Lessons for the Violoncello'.

7. Reinagle, *Sonatine*, 2nd movement: 1st position, stretched 4th finger, slow bowing on *cantabile* notes, strong/weak phrasing, *vibrato*.

8. Reinagle, *Sonatine*, 3rd movement: 1st closed position, triplets, bow distribution (two triplet quavers on a down-bow followed by one on a lighter up-bow), coordination.

9. Gretchaninov, *Morning Stroll*: 1st closed position, playing melodic lines, ensemble playing, simple *pizzicato*, learning to alternate between *arco* and *pizzicato,* preferably plucking with the index finger.

10. Gretchaninov, *At Twilight*: 1st closed position, playing *legato*, string changes, (*Vibrato*).

11. Gretchaninov, *One Winter's Night:* 1st position, stretched 4th finger, half position; shifting between 1st and half position, change of finger on the same note.

12. Schlemüller, *Scherzo* op.12/3: 1st closed position, bowing technique, string-changes, using a small amount of bow, short *staccato* quavers, tone quality in long notes, change of character in the middle section, playing *legato*.

13. Schlemüller, *Ländler* op. 12/4: 1st closed position, bow distribution, playing *legato*, emphasis on the first beat.

14. Stürmer, *Allegro giocoso:* 1st position, stretched 1st finger and stretched 4th finger, 'classical' style with modern harmonies and changes of mood.

15. Hindemith, *Easy Piece:* 1st position, stretched 1st finger and stretched 4th finger, once half position, ensemble playing, dialogue, changes of mood.

16. Heller, *Lalai*: 1st position and stretched 1st finger, rhythmic variations as written-out *rubato, cantabile* lines, dynamics, experimenting with tone colours, e.g. playing *forte* with a slow bow close to the bridge, *piano* with a 'breathy' sound and faster bow over the fingerboard, *pianissimo* very quiet, almost 'with a single hair', *morendo*, allowing the last note to die away.

17. Regner, *Von einem anderen Stern [From another star]*: first encounters with modern musical techniques, harmonics in 3rd position, with the 1st finger placed where the 4th finger would be in 1st position, playing the 3rd finger above it. Harmonics can also be tried out and played in higher positions.

18. Pütz, *Spiritual*: 1st closed position, regular (e.g. bars 1-8) and irregular bow distribution (e.g. bars 11, 12, 13). Option to play an octave higher in 3rd position from the 4th beat of bar 16 onwards; changing fingers on the same note makes it easier to experiment with a new position.

19. Wunsch, *Dorian Blue*: 1st closed position, swinging *legato* quavers – 'Blues' feeling, ensemble playing.

20. Koeppen, *Wind Song*: 1st closed position, once stretched 1st finger, bow distribution, bowing with a 'wandering stroke' (bars 12, 16, 24), retaking the bow with a slight shortening of the long note (bars 4, 8, 22, 30). Here a percussion group might join in. In group tuition students might take turns at playing one or several of the rhythms given, either on the cello or using their voices, to form an accompanying band. The bass line of the piano part may also be used as an additional cello part, either playing the rhythm given or with continuous crotchets (bars 9, 15, 19, 27 would have to be transposed by an octave). This piece could also be played with whole phrases shared out, e.g. as question and answer (changing over every four bars).

21. Koeppen, *Disco-Hit*: 1st closed position, stretched 1st finger and stretched 4th finger, alternating between stretched 1st finger and stretched 4th finger, working on rhythms. Variations could be introduced with clapping and shouting; the piece may also be repeated from the beginning several times, producing a number of verses. A percussion group (see *Wind Song*) could join in here. If a larger group is involved, some choreography could be worked out.

22. Koeppen, *On the Beach*: 1st closed position, stretched 1st finger and stretched 4th finger, syncopation, *glissando* to the harmonic in 5th position (optional), extension of the 4th finger like a shift in position (bars 21, 33). A percussion group (see *Wind Song*) might join in here, or in group tuition students might take it in turns to play one or several of the rhythms given, on the cello or with their voices, producing their own combination of sounds.

23. Kemminer, *Lord of Chords*: 1st closed position, stretched 1st finger, playing fifths, syncopation, building stamina – don't insist on playing through these too many times in succession, to avoid strain from difficult finger placements in the left hand and fatigue in the right arm. A drum could well join in here; the piece could also be played by a group of cellos, where the fifths could be shared between two parts.

24. Kemminer, *Los niños del Tango:* 1st closed position, stretched 4th finger, augmented interval between 4th and 2nd fingers – best played like a shift in position, *glissando* into 4th position (bar 25, optional), which might be introduced and tried out here; contrasts in character, dynamic and tone colour.

25. Kemminer, *Shana Tova*: 1st closed position, stretched 1st finger and stretched 4th finger, augmented interval, *rubato* in ensemble playing; *arco* and *pizzicato* sections might be divided between players in group tuition.

Translation Julia Rushworth